Before a Blue Sky Moon is really a series of three long poems that focus on a Chinese upbringing in Calgary. Moving through childhood, family history, losses and redemptions both spiritual and secular, the author examines the meaning of personal love. In these poems, father, mother and lover are always intertwined, searching for the "mystery of tides / violent attractions and physical bodies / that don't know why they give in."

Why all this grief and turning pale?
Don't look at me.
Like any face reflecting other light,
the moon is a source of pain.

– Rumi

Before a Blue Sky Moon

Weyman Chan

[handwritten inscription:] Calgary Nov 2/03

For Ken (Rivard) thanks for your ongoing friendship Hilles and encouragement. You & Robert have always been there for me during the quiet, desperate hard time. Thanks in so many ways, Weyman Chan

FRONTENAC HOUSE
Calgary

Quatrain opposite Title Page: from UNSEEN RAIN: Quatrains of
Rumi, translated by John Moyne and Coleman Barks © 1986 by
Coleman Barks. Reprinted by arrangement with Shambhala
Publications, Inc., Boston, www.shambhala.com

Quotation p. 60: from CHUANG TZU: The Inner Chapters,
A.C. Graham, 1989 (ISBN 0 04 299013 0). Unwin Hyman Ltd.,
London UK, W1V 1FP, p. 161.

The publisher and author have made all customary and reasonable
efforts to obtain permission from owners of previously copyrighted
material. In the event that any copyright holder has inadvertently been
missed the publisher will correct future editions.

Cover and Book Design by EPIX Design Inc.
Cover Illustration by Sam Weber.
Cover Concept by Weyman Chan

Frontenac House acknowledges the support of Alberta Foundation for
the Arts.

National Library of Canada Cataloguing in Publication Data

Chan, Weyman.
  Before a blue sky moon

(Quartet 2002)
Poems.
ISBN 0-9684903-5-2

I. Title. II. Series.
PS8555.H39246B43 2002   C811'.6   C2002-910155-7
PR9199.4.C42B43 2002

Printed and bound in Canada

Published by Frontenac House Ltd.
1138 Frontenac Avenue S.W.
Calgary, T2T 1B6 Canada
Tel: (403) 245-2491 Fax: (403) 245-2380
E-mail: editor@frontenachouse.com
Website: www.frontenachouse.com

1 2 3 4 5 6 7 8 9   05 04 03 02 01

for my parents
and their parents

Acknowledgements

Thank yous are never enough for those first teachers who got me writing – Susan Cutmore, Susan Hughes, Edwin Ernst, Lawrie Mack, Gloria Dalton, Faye Holt. Later on, Charles Steele, Chris Wiseman, Aritha van Herk, and Fred Wah would push me, kicking and screaming at times, in new directions.

My wife June helped language and desire to converge. Our daughters Janine and Stephanie are living proof.

Other loves: My siblings. Paulo da Costa. Pamela Boyd. Sharron Proulx. William and Deannie Cicon.

And finally, there's the Toi Sahn Dialect Committee on Correct Usage – Sharyn Toy, Jim Wong-Chu.

Some of these poems have appeared in a slightly different form in *Capilano Review, Filling Station, Alberta Views* and *Opium Magazine* (Portugal).

Contents

I give you back these animals

The religion of surrender

Crossing this planet to the next

I give you back these animals

You can't be born until you've eaten
                    all their bananas
and burned down their forest –
every chimp and toad either dead
or domesticated or in a glass dish.

You could read these words
while holding yourself still

say them again from memory
and they would only be riddled
with enough urgency
to hint of something brighter

like a full moon in the blue sky of May
which leaves no solid line or ghost
on your children's faces. The sun
is just as you dreamed it in childhood

the Niagara pooled for generations
below the crowning headwaters
combed back and cinched with a rainbow mid-air.

And you're happy
that the light here is the same
as you imagined it, word-embellished
or not, polluted
or not.
            There's a misty contrail
where the world leaves our senses
out of range and lonely
in their stunted reach.

Plain and simple, I wanted you.
        Wanted your eyes burning mountainsides,
        hanging sunsets that stop our flat earth
        from pouring over the edge.

I made a wish
rising up on dragonbacked karsts
        rumoured by joss smoke
        written on air

wanted the want behind casual talk travelling Guilin
        factory girls' thin fingers magicking
        threads of silk
        out of hot cocoon water

wanted Bruce Lee's hot sneer cooler than stars
        that croon indifference but still
        save the orphan girl when her mouth
        opens like a blue-veined slave.

See my mouth?
I'm telling you with blood
whose wires always lead
back to the heart.

The argument in my head was originally with Dad. He floats flowers out to her grave the first Sunday of March, *Hung Sahn* it's called. Means walk the mountain. Entreat the ancestors, rectify yourself. From my first visit to her grave at age five, I've always recalled blue sky, a shy slanted half-moon, and the four of us, giggling as we ran down the hill from the cable TV tower. Our strong, inevitable stepmother clutched her purse and was the first to spread the flowers and incense stalks and bow three times. Arms held rigid, palms clasped together. Three deep kowtows. The reverence is meant to conjure something, maybe a harrowing face, a starved entity, out of clean air and sunshine. These words I've harvested only decades later. Back then the only words that conjured anything for us concerning Mom were cable TV and *Hung Sahn*.

Sometimes, locating you is guesswork and time travel. On good days, it's finding the mood that fits, saying it sad without abdication. On bad days, it's like being frozen mid-air. I sat up in my crib, a crib with steel bars. You, in the pajamas of my sister, sat up, instantly protective of me from your own crib behind your own set of bars. The room we're in is an endless maw of beds, cribs with bars lined up. There's enough light to see your face, your tiny fingers touching one or two notes on a blue piano. Vena cava blue. Music blue. Just enough notes to pool the crying orphanage around our private awe of those notes, the clear-belled respite that toys bring.

You and I didn't cry. We spoke Chinese to each other, me two years old, and you barely four. I remember not knowing how to ask, Where are we? as if this would lead to the larger question. And you were calm, with both feet tucked neatly beneath your blanket, and you didn't mention Mom or Dad's name. The blue piano was enough.

I wanted you locked inside one word
        angel   translucence   mother
                wanted to travel more than one ether
after you died
      when all of a sudden you weren't there
      and my crying took in the row of cribs

temporary orphanage bars at night
here's the city   whispering
its toxic bloom down third avenue   hookers
                          like weeds
                  miasma and orgasm
        the city at rest only when its sunset
fills my throat eight beers later

        a long low hovering
        bruised heels pushed through t-straps
cutting tired   miasma and orgasm
            so heavy

    I'm thinking they've been pushed up on their tiptoes
    The asphalt warm like their nipples just from the mileage

Where do we go from here, baby. You're my moonlight
    my car window eye candy
      my smell and follow
        on stiletto pavement my headlights cross
the same Orphan Annie eyes though I want to tell my sister
          that we held the same toy piano between us

in that huge room of crying cribs end to end
we passed the piano between us
one or two notes back and forth
sparing ourselves the one missing thing
the hole in the sky the word that might swallow us

The floating of galaxies like strangers.
They match my distance as I invent
their orbits on a quiet street,
their million-to-one chance meeting
in this café
after I've searched them out in the night sky.

You are smaller and harder to find than the moon
whose faded circle pulls me
into the turquoise sky of my stepmother
which was steady as a mantra,
full of Chinese myth.

A maiden or queen flies to the moon
to escape her husband's anger.
Such a lofty leaving
if it were possible, would maybe teach us
about restraint.

Either that, or imagine a blue sky
blacked out with floating girls,
grandmothers, all women
tethered to a dream that pulls them up by the real.
They're more numerous than birds leaving
the knife-edge of winter

Oh she's a mean one. Oh she's a mean one.

Birthday cake. Her birthday cake. She's smearing it on the bed and walls of your room. None of us understand why. Later when you come home from A & W and Dad's at work, nowhere to defend you-his-flesh-and-blood against her, when I say to myself, Boy she's gonna get it. It started out so nice, morning at the breakfast table, when the birthday cake was presented. And you-his-flesh-and-blood begged to love her. We have nothing in our dialect to say *Love You* except *hun nee*, which is the more parental love, whereas *oi nee* is more conjugal.

Birthday cake. Sweet *hun nee* love that Oh she's a mean one failed to read. That Sunday morning at the breakfast table started out nice for a Mother's Day, which was when we celebrated Step Mom's birthday since she feared telling us the exact date of her birth, why? maybe superstition. Maybe we could draw on hexes, or bring back our first mother from the dead if we knew that. The birthday cake said not just "To Mom" but "To Our Mom." In red luck icing.

Then you gave her the birthday card in a white envelope. I didn't know why. You should've written "Mom" on the envelope, turned the glaring white into something else, a utilitarian envelope by virtue of having one plain word written on the face. Instead, she is faced with a blank white mirror into death. And if that weren't enough, you then had the nerve to wear jet black pants to work.

You come home. Get screamed at for two hours. I am sitting with my feet propped up above the gas fireplace, its low blue flames warming a day that has turned to rain. She climbs the stairs yelling, but will not enter the walls of the room she's desecrated. And you lie face down on your bed, with those dried but still oily rosettes, variegated crucifixes of icing, a day gone so bad, so wrong, that when Dad comes home from work, two in the morning, he will pull out your bed, start washing the walls. Will go downstairs, drag her out of his bed and hit her. Will climb back up the stairs, tuck his children in for the night, a change of allegiances will bring him back to us. Will bring our MaMa back to us.

He comes home. Gets into bed beside her. Our house is quiet.

Our house is.

You can't be born until you've eaten *kau-ngook*,
sliced taro root alternating with strips of pork back
steamed forever in a hot pot.

Eat mooncakes for the August festival wrap sweet rice *foong
cheng* nuts and egg yolk in bamboo leaf and steam it to a hard
four-cornered dumpling. Untie the string, peel back the leaf
and smell the sticky rice. *Doong*, we call it *doong*, a feeling like
dazed relief when Step Mom cuts a *doong* in half with string,
and my half has the yolk.

the silence is   my father   my stepmother
leaning   from the stairwell

of a broken house   house of spirits
bought and paid for

by their immigrant love   the moon
thready as a failing heartbeat

soon any time at all   they'll separate
be done with each other's pain
of leaving   Mom campaigns   for our love

"if I leave you can visit me anytime"

"oh no we'll stay with you"
my sister cries her eyes widening
with compassion or sugar

or whatever a mother can possibly be
when you don't and should have one.

I don't remember how we met but
you stay, caught up in our shared history
of rock cod, pan-fried in tomato ketchup
and served on those same vitrified oval dishes from old
restaurant days.

Why haven't you learned how to be tragic?
Outside of history, your parents raised you in a town
nestled in mountains, mornings so high that
waking up, you must have felt feathers instead of hair.

A mother who dresses you warmly
and loves you mid-air
before the playground roots you down
among the older children
who aren't Chinese but not separate either.

I want to love you but
see, the moods I wrestle into the shape of love
are all stolen.

From our mother tongue
down to these silk sheets that open to your back
I am nowhere near you, not even close
to being born a man
who knows himself or his fantasies
of complete dependence.

And soon, like all women
you will disappear

I wanted you not drowning but
waving those incense sticks
across the ancestors' names.
I thought you'd point this eight-sided mirror
against bad luck.

Instead, you use it to floss.

I grew up knowing I was half-celestial.
Above us, the moon's white rabbit
sat with mortar and pestle
grinding the elixir of immortality.

Step Mom reminded us of the moon holidays.
Don't wash your hair.
Don't wear black or white anything.
Don't wear ribbons of any kind in your hair.

I simply vanished behind her flesh-mask
while you grew up fishing in mountain streams.
You looked up and saw your heart in the same place.
I could never intervene
in any song of my own body
without spooking the ancestors.

Memory was somewhere that Chinatown, all Chinatowns, were born out of key words – shanty, exclusion, yellow peril, cheap labour. Migrant force. Dad used to bring me down to feel the wind and broken sidewalks of Chinatown. He'd just remarried and had taken the four of us back from our foster homes. Above the sunshine, a shy glass moon darted between skyscrapers.

He was so happy to hold my hand, to visit his friends who cut me a duck's wing from the grease-dripped carcass, roasted to a caramel-red glaze. Memory was Dad holding my hand, allowing my greasy hand to ply in and out between his fingers. He said to me, *If you ever want anything from me, all you have to do is call my name, Daddy, Daddy-ahh....* For two years, he'd waited simply to be here for me – and I'd grown up on him. I ran alongside him, jumped within his shadow, rhymed with it. Perhaps saddened that I couldn't recall what MaMa looked like, he offered himself that day as the unconditional father. His hand left my neck, the air filled with quiet blue traffic and the empty flash of their leaving. His face that day floated between something brighter and something sweeter. Memory was the way he walked, hand and eyes softened by wind and my breathing and Chinatown shared between us.

We were meant to grow to leave these things behind.

Eight years ago I waved goodbye
to a cousin in the town of Hoi Seng
near my father's birthplace along the Ghost River.

It was an earth that had turned
my revolutionary father away.

The land of his birthplace was no longer his
it was overrun by poplars instead of mango trees
and the *mook maing* trees of his childhood
whose red blossoms were the size of your head.

The animals he'd once eaten were also diminished.
No more ocelot, pangolin or owl –
magical creatures that hunted under a full moon.

Dad's appetite for their meat was left unsated
at the open market
where only the usual pig and chicken carcasses
dripped blood into curbside gutters.

"No damn good," he said.

I felt his ice age come again, his cool burn
for something lasting ended up at his mother's grave –
an extinction that only an overseas visitor wanted to see.
So my cousin for the next two weeks became his servant.

I didn't pretend to know him
he brushed his teeth with water
slept under sour cotton netting on a plywood board
he'd peel oranges at any hour of the day or night
throw the peel over his fourth floor balcony where
a pile of rotting garbage lay
on the corrugated tin roof of the marketplace below.

It was his servitude to my father that kept me from
looking into my cousin's eyes

He'd give Dad the umbrella while he soaked up the rain
and humiliation

He kept having to retrieve Dad's reading glasses and did this
even on the day when Dad stopped promising
he'd sponsor them to Canada

On the day we left China he just smiled and gave me his
stamp collection

I gave him a used tube of toothpaste after seeing that
toothpaste sold at the friendship stores here in 1990 cost over
twenty yuan, more than a week's wages

an old tube of toothpaste
standing wet and abused his hand gratefully accepted
the place we lived only one airplane flight away

I really thought he'd use my toothpaste

The blue sky is dark
now that you turn towards the leading edge of moonrise
where threads of night cascade
into underbellies, shadows.

I see a nodding hollyhock
shoot through the solid pea vine.
From here they seem melded together like hair.

I want to describe their loss of outline and depth
as they lean into that nightfall blue
leaning into the same darkness
that is the colour of night arrived at inside their flesh
and mine, we're all the same now
and my words to describe this
also fade to black.

Moonlight, rain down like the moon you are.
You can't be used to gauge anything
in three dimensions. My eyes
fall inward from the periphery, apprehending shapes
in a slow melting sense of urgency
until gravity itself seems flattened
to the pea vine's lattice.

I stalk through silent shades and outlines and the
unresolved space
high above earth where no love survives
without instinct and cunning.

We get married.
Right away we start to pull apart the cage
of what we thought love was
without the eight-sided mirrors and incense romance
of some domain that really was the moon kingdom's
unrecognizable edge   kisses misunderstood
when planted on the world
with all the wars remotely fought and lives torn apart
still everything   win or lose   should have
fallen in our favour

                              I came to you hurt and drained
of colour and days
only the night with you was worth sleeping for
the universe stopped
                    our eyes turned inward
from the opium ports   the lotus feet
              of shouting grandmothers

centuries
how we go on cherishing our past
with its white man's history of ownership
the world is what it eats
as I pull your breasts towards me
and push my veined belly against yours

My father named me after the Maoist revolution going on in his own heart. My name, 偉民, is *Wee-Meen* in Toi Sahn dialect. Means *great people*. Means there's an expansiveness in his pride and also privilege in loving the multitude through the chosen one.

He opened the World Café with my mom in 1958. The world like a spleen, a vague organ of loose tissues connected with veins pouring hope into him like cheap drink. She, straight from the rice fields of *Heng Ha*, whose English whirled with broken grace from her tongue, would be dead in eight years.

She left you and the four of us in 1966, when we barely knew the language. In 1990, when my cousin led us to your mother's grave in China, in the fields of rain and wet clay, that's what I remember: the walk along thin red clay furrows. Your sister my aunt walked ahead of us, carrying her sacrificial canon – bottle of rice wine, string of firecrackers to ward off ghosts, some roast pork from the butcher's. She balances like a dancer on the red clay furrows, walking quickly, pink umbrella raised. Servant of the house of spirits.

An old villager points his bamboo cane into the sheet of rain and after another five minutes we arrive. By then, Dad, we are holding you up. Your ribs are my ribs, heaving with broken sobs. I feel the force of her hands from the earth, this grandmother of mine whom you've only told me one or two things about. How she saved your life when you were a man of fourteen. How she died in 1962, waiting for your return. One or two breaths about her was all I needed to make sense of your howling nights, your rooftops and rivers of home. But I've known her only as much as I've known about my own mother. Which is why they are up there and you and I are down here worshipping.

Place and time were when my cousin and aunt spread out the small bowls and offerings. They waited until you finally spoke, for all of us and in communion with the dead:

MaMa. I, your oldest son, have returned. We are together now.
Everything is well. Lee-see. I am here and I bring you offerings.
Grandfather's grave is still somewhere among these hills. We will
find him one day. But we honour him here with you too. BaBa.
I, your oldest son, have returned. We are all together now.
Hum-tai, lee-see.

The words make and unmake me, past and future, inside and out, as you kneel before this wet earth your heart stands on, birthplace and beacon.

Longing to hunt the tastes you'll always crave, even when you're gone.

I will give you back these animals that open you to place and time:

Ocelot.   Pangolin.   Owl.

Sometimes when I visit
you study me out of the corner of your eye
re-visiting my failures
like old haunts

the moon is nothing to you
you've given her no special name or memory
she pulls nothing and draws on nothing
beyond your influence

maybe because you learned long ago that the only things
you can change are human feelings
the coronas of your own flesh and blood

words were everything to you
words like *moi-yoong*, good-for-nothing
you wanted them seeded in our appetites
a Pavlovian response to get things done

get rich   get renowned

we're too old now to be sucked in
our words glance off of each other
blunted by failure
to engage in shame

as we say our good-byes I pull you towards me
into my letting go
your refusals rising from sleep
like dreams on borrowed time.

Dad I failed to understand
how oracle bones can set down a peasant's path forever

how our word for man

connects with the word for large

connects with the word for heaven/sky

generations of eyes trained to see
a brushstroked man
high upon the belly of a weather inversion
and prayed to by ancestors
who hunted animal potions and animal elixirs
against human extinction.

They wanted everything connected to themselves.

Today I feel your eyes
rhyming my eyes and mouth to yours
waiting to complete the vertical brushstroke
between son and father –

it worked better back then
when your love for me was instinct
but then you stopped reaching out
and the alchemy of wild animals
kau-ngook and tomato rock cod
died out.

You haven't tried to change me or feed me, since....

You haven't come for some time now   it snows
rails at my bones
          cold blue stakes that rub   dead sparks
through my joints
     arthritic sun by day   snow at night

     snow at night   glistens on each drift
       foldless blue   except for a hushed path of ovals
like black eyes   from this light
you can't tell how deep the tracks go
or whose illusions fill them

You walked that path yesterday, remember?
Looking at it now
I can't tell whether they lead towards me or away

rich faithful moon   shine down
or sleep   shine down
or sleep.

The religion of surrender

The way we once ate

Our mealtimes I remember most. Elbows pressed together, this sense of Chinese, of a meal drawn out from taste to sphincter, day after day till it creates your whole life. As if I carry a homing pigeon's imprint. Forget the stars or the tilt of earth, it's there in Step Mom's wok, a cultural floating carpet of smells. Lunch time on Saturdays. Dad blaring his cassette tape of *Hoong Thlin Nooie*, or Red String Girl, I only know certain homonyms that approximate this singer's name, but Dad tells us she's very famous. Ah, the smell of simmered odds and ends, sliced fish maw with salmon heads, like no other. Bachelor train-tunneled, rusty tripod food, soup of deer bones and Lady's Slipper blossom, seasoned to form a tent inside one's mouth. Step Mom, shouting at us to line up with our rice bowls. We don't stand on ceremony here, lunch time on Saturdays, September leaves pulling down their gold, raining the air outside, and I know he's hung over by this light burning across the hardwood floor of our home, 528 eleventh avenue. Last night he drove out with the stars on his hat rim and this morning he's doused them on Step Mom's cold stare. *"Mao-ahk gong,"* he mutters when she asks him how much he lost. "Nothing to talk about."

I'm beginning to understand what he meant by that phrase – three or four generations of refusal there, the low kowtow eyes, bachelor shanty town, the barfly desolation, the coming-home absence of any wife or child to shine up to. *"Mao-ahk gong,"* I hear him intone solemnly, three or four generations sitting in a circle sharing flavours against one dead Chinaman for every mile of CPR track, or so the saying goes. Mushrooms sprung from dead wood. Black moss pulled from dead rock. The earth a scavenger's paradise when you're hungry. "Aiya! Ai-ai-ai!" Dad winces as he lowers himself to the head of the table, surveying the food in front of us, pressing down our happy table with his chef's elbows grieved to the bone, kitchen heat in his pores, the not letting go, the visible tracks leading back to his days as a starved boy face-down in a mud puddle, and a woman flying down to earth, live with salt and moon-pull before her face smacks the riverbed. It's like he wanted to say so many things, but food always managed to get in the way.

Snow poem

I want to write a poem about snow
and the naming of snow
in the word our Step Mom re-trained us to say
in Chinese –
thloot meaning snow –
as she held a piece of beef jerky out for us
to say each word of our mother tongue

in 1968 we were reclaiming
like daylight savings the tongue that would repatriate
our love for anyone who dared to marry our father
to save his four kids from the foster homes.

Dad and Step Mom talked about *Heng Ha*, the homeland:
Sah Vun, Thlum Gup, Bahk Sah
jeweled villages on a shepherd's path
to stone-hedged grave markers,
each one in the shape of an inverted omega,
carved into rainy hillsides.

They never saw snow until they came to Canada

> *if your eyes move with it*
> *the snow will hold still*
> *while the earth meets up with it*
> *never to own or to be owned*

Step Mom warned us about heaven, when we were bad.
There's a heaven, she'd tell us. *"Yu-ga hin."*
She had eyelashes that seemed
the perfect altar of warmth
to die on

snow is the one thing
that holds still while we float free
between lattice and rivulet
snow is the anchor of our moderation

but snow kept her alone in the house
constantly sweeping out the grey air
yelling at us to step back
when we walked in dusted with snowflakes

and years later on the morning
my mother-in-law died
her last eyes looking out
followed that gentle whiteout
it hushed her breathing and I wondered
how anybody could stand open-mouthed
looking upward
hoping to cradle-catch that illusion of falling
into its own vowel – its *no*,
negation, have-not of heaven
following the *s*

and if snow could be a poem about the body
when in other seasons a fish
could dream air out of water
or a tree could bend sugar out of light,
then snow would talk about disbelief,
its six-sided dissolution
in the millions
proving that the smallest touch lasts

why her, why this falcon-like fall
from recovery, only to believe with
all the science of your heart that all we have
is this body

this body taken by storms and dart frogs,
excoriations that bend leaves at night
with our children's voices crying for us

this body
caught in the middle distance
where life stops freezing or burning
and begins to know itself.

I skated on the river today
amazed that this distance could be mother to water
and that water could have made me

to remember a word like *thloot*
on a day like today where the sun spoke to me
like an old friend –

> *Yes I remember you when you left me yesterday*
> *and I've slept without you in the world*
> *anticipating nothing until now.*

Rain poem

In my dialect you say rain as *lok sui*, meaning falling water. My dialect is dying out. Old timers in Chinatown, pioneers who came from famine-stricken farmlands west of Canton City, are the only ones left. Only they know the self-sufficiency of growing vegetables in their own back yards and watering them with their own urine. In my dialect you say, *ngeem sui*, to drink water. If you are *geng hoet*, you're thirsty. Growing up, there was never enough milk so we had to *ngeem sui* when we were *geng hoet*. The point is, you forget that you're dying of thirst for a language that there's not enough of.

A window on the past

This morning we struggled with jars of jam, four burners and
the oven going. They tumbled out of your sterile tongs, one
third of the jam spilled, a portion of the domestic trinity lost.
Jazz clouds played on the sky outside as we stood apart,
waiting for those lids to suck in.

We laughed about it later, jam in our hair and kisses stuck to
our kids' faces to help them sleep better at night. I took off my
clothes and held you like I sometimes do for the moon, letting
its strange light shine its skeleton over mine – this mooncalf
devotion to pain, deflected and captured on you – I'm sorry.
You sense my withdrawal from the air, the tips of our tongue,
the roofs of our mouth. The not-saying that touches
everything.

Outside, jazz clouds play lightly across the moon's pink-eye.
Forest fire up north, I guess. It's been a dry October, one year
exactly since your mother died. Her gravid white eyes on a
linen face, I've nearly forgotten. I touch your hand and know I
belong to you. We ward off speech, words that fork the tongue
into half-truths that bypass the inner life. Our limbs catch fire:
be careful of your heart. Even a good heart can throw a clot,
unleash emboli like time's arrow

Candied plums

Her box of pain management
always in the garage next to his car tools:
first at 528 then at 972 where we moved to in 1980.

After his heart attack, Dad asked me if I remembered Mom.
"Three memories," I said. Dragging a toy duck or boat across
the living room while she sat there moaning in pain. She
comforting me after Dad nicked my ear during a haircut.
She in her hospital bed telling me not to drink so much pop.
I don't remember her face. I remember the soft white
Styrofoam coffee cup, its bubbles whispering to my lips on
the rim. And then I drink.

Inside the wooden box is a steel-tipped glass syringe, its
plunger frozen from the last dose. A half-empty vial of
morphine, septum-sealed. Date: Feb. 4, 1966. Three decades
has turned its liquid sepia-coloured.

"But you were only two years old back then," Dad says, his
voice breaking. I tell him I do remember. He asks me if I
remember this one: me, playing on Mom's back while she lay
half-asleep, dying. Me, rubbing her back here, and there, and
asking her in Chinese, "Are you better now? Are you better
now?" And Mom telling me, "Oh yes, Oh yes," while she
cried softly.

Sometimes the heart leaves you for years. It takes years to
figure where it's gone, and why.

Dad never played with us when we were growing up. He was in the garage fixing his cars, or smoking there so Step Mom wouldn't see him. When our relative plunged herself over a bridge, he told us that she died beautifully. Then he retreated to his garage.

I bet he loved the sight of that closed wooden box, that once held the candied plums Mom parceled out one by one, sweet kisses, each one.

Written on water

She was a distant aunt whom we called *Gun Goo*. Honorary
name after she jumped or fell off Centre Street bridge at first
snowfall, "the dead that fly towards sunset" reminds me of
what she did which became the noun *Gun Goo*. We were
teenagers I said to my sister don't pull a *Gun Goo* the Bow
River beneath us river meaning carried away forever flippancy
helps when everything surrounds like a circular waterfall
tipping you towards its edge but the river is there and we
don't owe it anything

I brought you here where she and I stood back then and you
said nothing among the wild rose and Indian paintbrush and
your sweater billowed like blown glass at the end of a sentence

Angel

ever since the earth found its moon
desire has filled our sleep

look now her sweater blown over her shoulder my
feet tiptoed in winter socks prayed to her wrist bones

we fell hard onto pillows from Mecca

my father, a boy of fourteen, is fallen over in a monsoon storm

see his shoulder poles pinning him face down

but he's wondering still why he and his mother sold their
water buffalo for the rice sacks drowning him and why
starving he can't get up

then he is lifted out of the mud piggy-backed home on wings,
sharp shoulders, ribs of a walking skeleton

A poor bachelor boy dreams
in a foreign land

He dreams of woman
as time and space kneel above him
she must be sung to
caught and then caged in the language of birds
but Dad had no poet's vocabulary in this new language
he learned English built a restaurant around it and waited

she flew in one day and bore him four children
and flew away.

After she died he seemed to long for simpler pleasures.

He was a boy running through poplars, hillsides, endless forest
decay. He found a small lake, plunged into it and found that by
using a bamboo pipe he could gather small carp. He'd surface
with one hand stopping the end of the pipe – enough fish
inside to keep his mother and sister alive for one more day.

He used to fish and hunt a little. There's one photo of Dad
and Mom in 1958, before any of us were born, with a trio of
fish lucked out of an icy pond.

In 1940, there were salamanders and frogs, deer in the forest,
and home-flocked clouds overhead. And something else close
to his heart – a jet black oriole would sing for him, dart from
the farthest rice fields and land on his hand. After he was
carried home by his emaciated mother, his near-death changed
him. He'd hunt those deer. Kill anything for food. He
bartered with the Japanese – offering opium resin for rice.
They'd pat him on the head as if he were a rare, silent thing
about to vanish for the trees.

Three studies of the human torso

1.

He cried into his starry blanket
as if sadness were an occupation

the river he cried mirrored drowning
words that couldn't say what his future might be

he meets himself years later
and finds he hasn't changed

in a place far enough from earth and people he was a boy
calling his water buffalo back home to its leash

2.

Mom did you fold laundry to extinction diapers body forms
repeated along the same folds did you give in to the heap of
arms and legs thinking that the world is too big a concern for
it these are not tangled humanity from a gas chamber are not
strangers but your four children

the white blossoms from the orange tree the oranda in the fish
bowl the progress of evolution which carried you along like
light that dusts through linen surprising the room with a
diffuseness which can't be made brighter or compared to
anything but the source of light itself a reason for the life you
found here feeding us rice and cleaning up our shit

my own daughter I hold her like a singing voice I've always
known for my own even when at times I was lost letting my
words overcome feeling because I want to reach for you as my
daughter reaches across to me and over my head for the
curtain where she senses beauty on the edge of shade and light
in motion and how its changing is a thing taken for a ride
through her tiny hands

you would've taught me how to survive everything that I say
or think seen through your flower print dress you would've
made me clothes sewn together scraps of light reflected from a
fish bowl you would've taught me your eyes that open like
Dad's favourite flower the night blooming cereus

3.

Grace is something I can't explain
divined sensed spoken to alone in a car on a dark road

you sit beside me in another life you who died at age 33

you sit beside me old   a mother I dote on
I take you with me everywhere

I watch your mouth like I used to watch the hems of your
dress

I watch your lips trembling
with a lifetime of spoken comforts

me my fantasy of you even if you can't hear me it's a beautiful
senseless day

        I'm sick of these tall trees bent over me when
all I want is you

            so simple

                you

mom of mine sun warmed mouth and hem your shade is like a
religion

of surrender which until now has been invisible

                        to me

Roof of heaven

The day Dad told us that *Gun Goo* killed herself
I froze an image of her walking with her cane
up Centre Street to our house
the stories she could tell of Chinatown
her pockets full of White Rabbit candy

he said that she had jumped out of sorrow
for the pain in her leg
that it was for the best
at least she left her choice there in the iced rocks below.
He had no choice about the way his mother
peeled him back from the mud and discord

Now old and resting
in the calm of the deal
made between themselves and the tea they're offered

the ancestors aren't just a word
stuck like candy to the roof of the mouth
they look down on every pyramid
of oranges every sweet meat
joss smoked sun spilled over newspapers
good luck ribbons and a triptych moon
slung overhead

and this loss which pursues me
has also deepened my pursuit of love
as if loss created love
out of memory tied off at birth
separated and left
bleeding for its own generation

White rabbit

I've been drawn towards the mystery of tides
violent attractions   bodies
that don't know why they give in

this moon, the scientists say
is an accretion of leftover debris
from an earth torn into
by a passing planet four billion years ago

so the first creatures to become extinct
lived before there was a moon

the moon draws your face near
just as it still draws countless meteors
towards itself and away from earth
saving us from extinction by fire

and so I've wanted to simply watch the glow
around your head that has its own reasons
for capturing me here

aimed between distance and disappointment
before my eyes adjusted
to this warm lamp at night
and your barely touching skin drawing me in.

Crossing this planet
to the next

Five senses

Sleep fills me like land
before civilization. Before I've lived enough
to consider someone else the source.

Back then all things reflected themselves
and those who faced death praised the harsh night
that invented them

Sleep fills me like land and already
I've promised to return
trusting in that moonless river
that drains light from memory

Suddenly the dream is.
My face and mouth slide seamless into another life's name
like one of Escher's prints
showing how sea birds rise out of the dark waters
even as diamond-shaped gaps of air
between these birds descend and form
the tessellated shapes of fish in that same water

as if every element has its life and a shadow life
married to it
and clarity comes
as a blurring
not of firmament or space
but of perspective.

We must call down the headhunters.
Dim the lights and disgorge our five senses.

Black out
to begin again.

Winter's trees

1.

A boy aged ten is walking home from the library.
He stops at the lights of Twelfth and Edmonton Trail.
The afternoon stands high on his shoulders –
he's in a splendour that up until now seemed
forgotten in the branches of trees
the crimped furrows of cloud overhead

this year his heart of defense has opened
to girls' mouths that are wet and desirable
they can say your name and hold you to it
a touch that moves you out further
into anxious running sweaty neck armpits
his body tempting the lights of Twelfth
and Edmonton Trail

out of breath imagine being struck
by a car what a thrill to think fast regretless death
at age ten wow I must be growing up
thought the boy.

The freeing of sound
is in a bird's cry is whispered
in the pages of a book of chess he holds
or if he cocks one ear into the breeze
and empties his body for the air to whistle through.

2.

Winter's rind not about to peel
not about ice kept warm by a white blanket
and not about him either

the naked trees
are hinged wrists locked finger upon finger
and frozen in an upwards reach
and he wants to know
what if anything these trees are saying
and where gesture without emotion leads
when you are old and alone and supposing
that the sun still walks with you as a shadow
trails the earth just to clarify
that you are of this earth
old and alone and supposing
that the winter trees are pulling groundwater
and light together into a sculpture
that saves the air

how complex these wrists
that seem formed by air itself
in the very lightness of a theme that
leaves you longer than any shadow
moving with you into old age
and as you move with it the sun does too.

The winter trees have summoned you.

3.

"Your sons and grandsons are not your possessions," says
Chuang Tzu. "Heaven and earth lend them to you to cast off
from your body as an insect sheds its skin."

When the boy was saved in the flesh
the heart had to follow
like a swimming reflex
he tried to get past those dreams
of drowning

he had to outgrow dying and tie himself off
at the belly button
with the phrase, *naing see hai kao*

which means, back then it was the way things were
so the boy as a man kept his childhood breath-choke

separate from today's easy air
its aspens meaningless

its skyband Chinooks
harrowing all shadows down
to a line of flame that would never cut through
his hollyhock hedge

4.

The trees were waving at him
off and on throughout his life only
he didn't know it.

I first noticed them
from the quiet sky of my bedroom window
when words first took me up
in the skin of a rocket

but when my mother died he stood at age three
before a spruce tree at the foster parents' house
in the height of summer breathing
in the deep musk green shade

wondering where she went
and later on when life was drawn
slowly around his knees
the trees around him were still waving

and when he learned to take down prey
with a kiss
and lie down along their vertebrae
somehow my flesh made sense of the movement

of clouds shaped by trees
that shaped the breaths that shaped my lungs
as if trees were a memory that
the earth and sky made just for me

to realize that I could bear
the blue sky moon's witnessing
that where she was and where heaven was
didn't matter
and that everything about my self was all right.

And the trees waved on
like birds living in haiku
above the first frost –
the trees and I loved him,

and he knew then that their sway green branches
were his,
their genes so old that they were
our ancestors to light.

The smallest difference

The botanist names this open-spaced ridge *montane*.
He doesn't mean mountain: montane is the height of ground
above the foothills but below the subalpines.
I'm twenty-six at the time, daydreaming of stories that make
good novels. We're all good Christians venturing into
Kananaskis, affirming God, our bachelor servitude and how
our calling reminds us that we are here.

In the clearings beneath lodgepole pine there are blossoms,
pale coral root, twinflower with its rose-coloured trumpets
that hang in doublets from a wick-like stem.

"Linnea borealis," he calls it. Named after the "father of
taxonomy," as I learned to call him in grade seven biology.

"And borealis as we all know comes from Borealis, the Greek
god of the north wind," adds the botanist.

I'm amazed that not only does he know his montanes,
but that he shares an apartment downtown with his blue tangs
and starfish and his Duke Ellington. He holds a small sprig of
feathermoss to his chin as he speaks.
We follow the path between Cataract Creek and the
Cretaceous. I find a squirrel to feed and photograph. He
gathers us to the damp humus between two trees.

"Look," his lips so engorged they're blue. "Northern bastard toadflax."

I see a tall, spindly weed. Some star-shaped petals – five, white, unremarkable.

"Actinomorphic, polypetalous, epigynous."

I could tell that he lived for the naming. A sorrow for the living that he must anchor with precision, naming the smallest things so they won't be grieved for after the faithful are raised, and all that grows is fire.

Sunsets like bullets

Without you it's as if the sky behind me disappears
without your face
birds and ships pass through me without
charting the stars they came from
words no longer drift or turn to auras
your bracelets slip off one by one
and do not shatter as you pass.

The trees grow little tombs around their seeds
now only fire can spread them
white aspens make black shadows
rain on a lover's neck bends light
away from her body back towards the air.

I imagine some lovesick monk from across the ocean
naming this bush Silverwood Artemesia
after a woman he couldn't have or hold
so he must search for her
and kneel in the forest
at the hem of her garment
while his own heart severs him

just as day and night must be kept apart
by the smallest bend in earth.

Crossing this planet to the next

He wasn't the first beggar I ever saw
as I looked up from my notes on cell biology
but the morning grass lifted him
as our bus pulled into campus.

He wore a fishing hat, a puffy brown ski jacket
with large down-filled squares
from the seventies. His walk was a shuffling run
and his face was dark and small. Himalayan, I thought.

Across his shoulders a long bamboo pole
joined garbage bags at either end
filled with soft drink cans. The black bags didn't jostle
but seemed to float over the small rise
he emerged from as sunlight behind his back

the sunlight through our bus window
straight into our eyes

you see him and think, Yes
he has crossed this planet to the next.

Poem for pessimists

The act of opening a newspaper
is a crossword for you
but for me, the headline reads
More Women Than Men Turning Away from God –
the Peruvian magenta scarf I gave you
lines the easy chair, warm against your back.

Undescended Genitalia in Mexican Village –
your cheeks deepen with contentment
in your circle of close friends
whose recipes are lived out by their preparation.

Melanoma Cases Skyrocket –
their pigments scatter with autumn
rolling claw leaf-sounds
which might clarify the issue
for those of us who think
that children born with one torso and two heads
must accept Jesus together
or else be split apart
at the Lake of Fire.

All Saints

Why am I sitting here
immune somehow

     the boy and his mother tied to a tree
at first it was thought   on a night like tonight

hallowe'en   they were lovers   I ran with her on
my shoulders   our laughter gentle   frozen after the night
fog lifted   extricate   lash marks
          writhings
         she worried about her legs getting tired

tortured dying forced into making love with stars watching
you on your last night alive into the backbone of your own
baby the very air you breathe purity itself

I worried that maybe she wouldn't get enough candy because
we started out too late already some lights down the street
have turned off doorways dark pumpkin lanterns snuffed out

the men who did this friends exhorting old glories deep in
their throats if only everyone could be a country pure and
without blemish

     serbkosovar   hutututsi   chinesetibetan

     Reese's Pieces Oh Henry Skor Lifesavers Sweet Tarts

Bowlfuls of candy spread out and sorted like loot over the
living room carpet. My daughter falls asleep in her Sailor
Moon costume, superhero for one more night.

The men who do this, on a night as delicate with thrill as ours. Why do I sit here with my mouth full of candy when out there, nothing but trees grow, roots spread out in memory. Peeling bark roped into witnessing, wearing the tourniquet of soft bodies that sucked in and hardened like the weight of snowfall.

Kafkaesque

I'm the one who enters as a way of leaving
a way of letting go

I enter her like boredom
reverses pity into the will to dominate

it's easy to become the cadaver
whose head snaps back to release the wad
to wonder at the transformation
of a nightmare like Kafka's
which builds its own labyrinth.

No wonder that insect he wakes from dreaming
to find that he's become
is a scavenger and a shadow
that you cannot expose to light

an ordinary feared pest
taking you to damp corners
infused with calm terrorism
where strychnine is the mystery poured from grails.

He does not write about brides in a garden
or about his father's naked hairy back
his making of the desires of flesh is jagged with bones
not the surface that reflects only surfaces.

Beneath layers of civil clothing
beneath stacks of newspapers that cloud
memory with fact and distance
he is drawn to cruelty in trick positions.

The uselessness of sleep is the torn veil
rice paper thin
of being accepted in polite society
with eight stuttering legs.

Sitting so hawk-like

beneath the shade of your own making, your perfect dream
must be a back yard full of apple trees. We have little in
common, except that our mothers died without us. Over the
years I've seen your cut fingers bleed into the recipes, sweet
and sour pork, bean thread noodles written aromatic with
black fungus for good luck. My hands also bleed easily and
sugar cane tastes of the way you sliced it with a giant cleaver.
Mouth full of splinters, the juice of it spills back to land, back
to village, trees before the making of men, a boy's love of
heights with each branch climbed and left behind –

he left you and your mother and your three brothers and
sisters you were only fourteen in 1940 ploughing the field with
your water buffalo and never enough food and we Chinese and
our trains and dynamite tied in with not quite slavery but the
blue skied promise of a hometown girl when in this country
you sent what little you had back home to your mom already
one of your brothers dead of starvation and the youngest sold
for money men stripped of language and exhausted but when
your father did come back you were sixteen in the rice field
and there he appeared in the sunset eyes turned up not
looking at anyone except to thread himself towards the
mountains he took the advance money to farm a neighbour's
land and in those two years spent everything and all there was
to do was let him die at home with uneaten portions of rice at
his bedside

– your face soothes me with its anxiety when I visit you in
Chinatown to read your heart medicines or open the window
blocked by an oversized orange tree. Stampede Wrestling
blares from the TV. You offer me peace through your delicate
health, and I take it whenever I can.

Directory

I watch him eating peanuts with beer over a spread-out sheet of newspaper. Headlines and shells disappear and he's a child sitting quiet next to his mother and they are both starving, ankle joints swollen and they could be near death. Sitting here with him 58 years later, he tells me how he chose my English name. He looked in the phone book to find a name whose spelling approximated the Chinese sound of it: *Wee-meen*. He finds the surname Weyman, and the name sticks.

A name at a glance can awaken a lifetime. Names can bring back an old lover, the adored but forbidden one, the one whose voice catches us in the amber of a single day. He says my name and I know myself. I say Dad and his pain is mine. Luckily, I've inherited my father's heavy sleep that lets things slide. He would cry for the money he'd gambled away, but after a good night's sleep he'd be all right, a little drunk maybe, every step balanced between two waves, as if his weight on this land if he weren't useful enough would capsize him back to China.

Vegetable garden

Twice a day, Step Mom helps out with his ritual. Using tin
bucket and saucepan, Dad dilutes the stored urine. I remember
peeing into those vinegar jugs, kept in the bathroom. My
sisters didn't have to. Only us boys. Those white vinegar jugs
that got so heavy and warm as you filled them up to their
hollow handles. Sometimes the smell was too much. Some
days I couldn't lift and pee at the same time. Now Dad ladles
the urine-water lovingly over snow peas, bok choy, spinach
and gai lun. Flies storm around the leaves that will appear days
later on our kitchen table, piping hot in oyster sauce or with
thinly sliced beef.

He belongs to himself best in his garden, hours planning
which apple stem to graft. Step Mom allows only certain apple
trees to be used, allows herself the luxury to criticize, knowing
his rage and how it spurs him on, lubricates the sun, turns him
into evening faster, lips parched, too tired to complain about
her food preparation.

Pronouncing his back ache curable and fixing him in the
doorway of her eyes as a thing accomplished and deserved to
this day because she stuck by him, Step Mom addresses him as
you. Take your shirt off, *you*. She doesn't see him as a lover or
husband, no damn way. A bowl of cool water boiled yesterday,
with a ceramic spoon dipped on edge. She holds the spoon's
dripping edge over Dad's bare back and scrapes. *Gut hoen*, it's
called, meaning scrape the sweat.

Beads of sweat billow out of Dad's face in the next half hour. She etches him with stunning red welts herringboned down either side of his spine and shoulder blades taking his wars to armistice and throwing his body to the mercy of a voice, a spoon's edge dipped in pain. He feels it right up into the roots of his hair.

Failure to write home brings mercy

After Dad's long crossing   thirty-three days by boat
the Chinese writing in his sky   seems remote
and the order of things
burnt out by expansion constants

he had left China   with a promise to his mother
who kissed him into the son's duty
he mistook for his manhood
he said that he would return to her
but how does a Chinaman return
except as money in proxy   a betrayal of wives
of new roots set down in *gwei law* country
contrary to matchmakers and widows
who say   the end is always tragic

It's like the story he told me of a Chinatown beggar
who could cure the pandemic flu of 1918.
He'd give his patients herbal soups
gut hoen them twice a day
feed them pork instead of chicken.
But he dies of exhaustion
while saving many of his people.

A saint in Dad's pantheon can reap
the whirlwind in a bowlful of rice

look song, gew song, yeet

six pair, nine pair, one

look song, gew song, ngee

six pair, nine pair, two

hao thloo-song ngeet

good auspicious day!

hao thloo-song ngeet

good auspicious day!

An old grandmother's chant, 1969

Small hands

Somewhere high up between trees and stars he's finishing off chapters, closing books on himself, sentencing to rest those ambitions that are no longer anyone's. He'd wanted me to become a doctor, to fenestrate healing through my eyes, as if I could somehow take him back to his mother who was struck in the head by village thieves and died slowly over the next fifteen years, intelligence seeping out, fine filaments that undo themselves. I would tell him about failed muscles, failed eyesight as it happens, the shitting reflex as it happens, get him through the witnessing. Then I'd listen to his complaints of the heart and likewise ease his own slow passage.

However we choose to meet each other, I'll be at an open market in Chinatown seeing an old face eyeing barbequed carcasses through the glass. He will sniff at the golden red skin, think back on tastier pangolins, owls, the supreme sweetness of dog meat, he will walk stooped with a cane. A silver V hairline retreating in the distance. Dad! If it's early I'll see him holding wrinkled hands behind his back, his outdoor slippers scuffing out a dime on the road. Safe passage to the dirt floor he slept on as a boy back home.

And here the old people walk and laugh, their remaining days sweetened brushstroke by raindrop down Chinatown streets in the body of a duck hung drip by drip beside slabs of braised pork. *Watch out for Small Hands*, the sign says, small hands meaning pickpocket in Chinese. The tree-cutting rush of a city grown beyond its sage brush valley at night the corners of each house lit from inside dreams lighting up the constellated bedposts of children, whose upbringing will never collapse them through the dirt floor to pariah, won't change their portion of fence and patio and these small hands which in the West means delicate feminine submission or when raised up in warning couldn't fend off a coyote if they wanted to, yet these delicate small hands of widows, ordering bean paste rolls, pork buns eaten at their apartment windows overlooking the

frontier city within a city, country within a country, are strong
enough to have survived the beck and call of husbands the
push of children the indignant fetus

I see his hands that are now above suspicion and official peril
status to the citizenry, cracked and sometimes trembling a
cloud of cigar smoke around his neck. I'll think of telling him
something he truly doesn't know. Like, what a strange and
lovely country we live in, Dad. Daddy-ah. BaBa.

These streets have their heartbeat merchants by day, high
heels by night. He walks by storefronts of the old standbys.
Hung Fung grocery. Gin Sung grocery. Silver Dragon. His
favourite has always been King Ying, now known as Golden
Inn. After Mom died, he would go to King Ying. The husband
and wife who ran that restaurant would – I don't know. I see
him stirring a few drops of morphine into his morning coffee.
A cure for the invisible ache. I see him shedding tears while
talking about her. What would he say about her, and how
would the proprietors at King Ying comfort him?

A celebration

We're digging into a cream roll from Chinatown when the phone rings. Telephone in Cantonese is *en-wah*, or "electric voice", whereas in Dad's Toi Sahn dialect it's *hum-thlin*, or "the crying line", Step Mom's on the phone. She can't find her eye drops. She's losing memory fast, and has reverted to the Cantonese she spoke growing up in Hong Kong as a child. At first, we believe she's forgotten that today is Chinese New Year's. The dialect of my father's people is steeped in superstition. In his part of the country you don't visit relatives on New Year's. You don't phone each other – spirit voices that summon you through magic receptacles, aiya! And contact with anyone outside of family is bad luck.

Tonight, Step Mom has forgotten what she and Dad had taught us. She asks us to come over right away. When we do, she's wearing pajamas – brand new pink ones. She hands out the *hoong bao* – red envelopes containing money – to my children. She's talking non-stop and we barely understand her. She entertains us until the fireworks go off over Chinatown. Their bright filaments reflect across my mother's glasses. She mouths the word for firecracker – *pao joong* – and I've never seen her lean so far from the window to find something out there that was once hers.

Inventory

My mother-in-law brought me a language not newly born but fully grown in her wild, lilac hedged garden. Thorned *geet-du* bushes thrived alongside rows of snow peas, or *thloot-ow*. Everywhere, *gai lun, yu toy, thlai yeng toy:* they all sprang up on their own. A large corner shrub of rhubarb she called roo-bahb.

Inside her house, a special kitchen cupboard held yellow-brown roots called *fook-seen*, lovingly wrapped in paper in a wooden box. There were fox nuts, packaged *geet-du* berries which she'd dried twenty years ago, herself. And three different varieties of ginseng.

One plastic bag held some black seeds, roots, lily flowers, and a small dried out turtle sucked into its shell. The sinews of its legs and neck were like translucent honey. My mother-in-law named everything and explained their purpose and value.

I wrote nothing down. I wasn't sure at the time as to why I was being told this.

I know now, and I miss her. I miss her for the too-late gesture, her effort to pass on information about healing that was supposed to help, but which she never used on herself. Otherwise this cupboard of treasures, of age and secrets and things to tell, wouldn't have been full enough to tell us about things Chinese – remembering these simple elements whose power to cure extended the riches of her day into ours.

When we spoke the same language

there's a fragility my love
to nerve and muscle
the bones of my story
scattered beneath layers
of fathers who've come and gone

where nerve came before muscle
and first thoughts
flamed in and out
blues and oranges
sounding out the bell
of a jellyfish

colour is just my nerves pleasing themselves

so here we are
at the end of our diaspora
numbed by this body
of nerve and muscle
and language-locked hands

evolution's trick
is not to rely on gods and quick escapes
but to change where I kiss you
on the intimate red strap
the impressionistic eyes

where "broken shoe" in Chinese
is *lun hai*
which also means
"worn-out vagina"

and a divorced woman
is called a broken shoe

heels tipped over pleasure
to the point
of self-laceration

what do we do with our culture
its glorious history its
disposable gender
its sex differential

set in nerve and muscle
the world's greatest population
made fragile over
what it is to be happy?

The end of grace

We forget that this has all happened before. That evening
when looking up outside our atmosphere and beyond the
asteroids, a string of broken moon tore its way towards Jupiter.
We couldn't see anything, but knowing what was happening
far away somehow turned the imaginary into an event, so we
pretended to be gods walking through Edworthy Park,
remember? Noticing every change in the warm night, as if ten
thousand years had passed. As each star appeared we held
hands and yelled, ten thousand!

Something about that night still affects us, uncatches our step
or slows down an apple. Gravity is still seduced by the drop of
your braid and how it undoes itself. But time is flown by birds
wintering south, birds that remember the return compass and
the moon's winging it, to travel in a blood rush like that with
one eye tuned to nothing, no ground just a reason for life that
escapes its own nest of places.

This has all happened before, and you have always been high
above the blue of my tongue, the withdrawal, the win and lose
of staggering, making love to change solitude, proving that our
senses must rehearse their part in the world to come. And the
world to come follows the new day, always different, always
half-written and half-spoken, no matter if I think of your
breast in the same way.

Once again, the ice age doesn't matter. The trees lean no differently from yesterday. Airplanes come and go refusing no one. I carry heat from this cotton sleeve lifted off the fireplace. I burn my wrist against your neck and watch your spine mime out a word for it. We journey to another day, save some light on the window sill, your glasses next to mine. The smallest things we have in common are what bind the earth to our feet, and wishes to our language. After the sheets settle and your breast is once again simply a breast. After you lie down with one arm under your neck, marbled breastbone like sculpture that you let yourself repeat thousands of years later. It's then that I memorize us, together, marbled June sunset irresistible to poetry that lets go of nothing, and you let the earth go. Your body rises out of paper or alabaster as I fall to catch you.

Comb

If I comb your hair to remember
you
then I keep the child you once were
for time is a living body
grandmothered through touch

If I comb your hair with water
then starfish and seafarers will free
themselves
and the exploded plane over Lebanon
whose rain of human flesh
scattering like birds in flight
will piece our own lives
back together again

because your hair is long
enough.
The comb slides through
where tides and voices move you
beyond memory

your hair's river washes
clean all the living body's wreckages
and through your hair the poured window
throws its light
into my eyes

you see my eyes and think Yes
I too have crossed that planet
to the next

Weyman Chan, who lives and works in Calgary, is married with two daughters. His poems and short stories have been published in several Alberta journals and anthologies over the past 15 years. His poetry also appears in *Many-Mouthed Birds: Contemporary Writing by Chinese Canadians. Before A Blue Sky Moon* is his first book.